The Authority of the Believer

A Disciple Maker's Manual

By Paul Jinadu

Introduction

The spiritual authority of the believer and who we are in Christ are among the most urgent truths every Christian needs to know. We then can live successful, purposeful lives in this modern world. He who knows his rights in Christ can live above circumstances, use the name of Jesus effectively, and be in a position to help those with various problems.

This book shows the Christian how to be free from the snares of the Devil and live above his power. It shows the importance of words, and how to obtain daily victory through confessing the living and powerful Word of God. Key scriptural issues are taught to ensure that you, the reader, become aware of your rights, responsibilities, and privileges as a believer filled with God's Word, God's love, and God's authority!

Rev. Paul Jinadu
General Overseer
New Covenant Church
London, UK

Contents

Contents (continued)

1. AUTHORITY over the DEVIL

One of the tactics of the Devil is to make out that he is a remote, ugly, and terrifying figure. By so doing, he slips into people's lives unawares through the back door. He has always given a false impression of himself as a horrific person with horns, long pointed ears, and a forked tail. The truth is that he deviously blends into everyday life and events so that he is not noticed, except by the most discerning.

The Biblical Picture of Satan

He is said to appear "as an angel of light." He can easily deceive because he seems to be familiar and friendly. He hasn't changed since he appeared to Eve in the Garden of Eden. Then he was in such a familiar form that Eve did not suspect anything diabolical. Had Satan appeared to Eve as a horrible figure with frightening features, she would no doubt have shied away from him. He appeared as a serpent, one of the creatures Adam and Eve had dominion over. In fact, it was Adam who gave it its name.

When Satan tempts us to do evil, he uses familiar and even desirable objects or activities to lure us away from the safe haven of the will of God. Most people would run away from temptation were it not so desirable. Eve was so comfortable with the serpent that she held a long conversation with it. Since it was just she and Adam with all these animals in the Garden, they must have had a way of communicating with them, which we would find incredible today.

At his sinister suggestion she took and ate the forbidden fruit. He had managed to convince her that he was more on their side than God was. Let's face it, the serpent was in the Garden long before Eve came out of Adam's side. It was easy for him to convince Eve that he knew a thing or two, and thereby lured her into his trap. Don't think that he has changed. He uses the same tactics to deceive people today. He is still the greatest counterfeiter ever known.

The Devil was a beautiful angel once. Perhaps the most perfect and beautiful creature God ever made. He is described as "the bright star of the morning." Perhaps one of the reasons for his downfall was his pride in his great beauty and perfection. Today he still attracts people to his side through beautiful things. "The lust of the flesh, the lust of the eye, the pride of life" are all ways in which Satan deceives people into worshiping him and neglecting their souls.

We are Surrounded

People are rubbing shoulders with Satanic agents—demons —almost every day, quite unaware of their damaging effects and diabolical operations. The average man on the streets has no means of detecting demonic activity. It's not spooky and sending goosebumps down your spin. They work on a spiritual plane.

But there is a way their operations can be detected. The Bible says, "We are not ignorant of Satan's devices," By the gifts of the Holy Spirit we can find them out and deal with them with the power God has given to every believer. Often, though, they are best left alone and ignored, as they have no power over a Christian who knows who he is in Christ.

Whenever I sense that demonic forces are working in a situation, say, for example, during a heated argument, I usually try to leave the place. Demons are capable of turning a simple disagreement between two people into a spiritual battleground. The sad thing is that some people give room to the Devil to inflame the situation until you have a major crisis on your hands. One man died just because he was trying to separate two friends from fighting. Suddenly one of the men picked up a bottle and accidentally smashed it on the head of the peacemaker. He bled to death on the spot. These men could not control their temper until tragedy struck. Lack of self-control is surely an ally of the Devil.

Satan is a Liar

Satan is a liar and the father of lies (See John 8:44). He not only tells lies, but is able to make people believe them. When the Devil is telling you a lie, two things happen. First, you won't know the voice of the Devil; it would sound just like your inner voice. Secondly, you won't be able to tell the lie from the truth. Confusing, isn't it? Here is a Biblical example: At Ramoth Gilead, Ahab, the King of Israel, wanted to go to war to reclaim some lost territory. On the one hand, his trusted prophets unanimously prophesied victory and encouraged him to wage the war. On the other hand, a lone prophet prophesied defeat. Naturally Ahab went for the majority, which this time around were all influenced by a lying spirit. He was made to believe a lie, which led eventually to his death.

Satan is a Pretender

The Devil pretends to be a shepherd of our souls, but Jesus

exposed him in John 10; he is come only to kill, steal, and destroy the sheep. If only the world of unbelievers would wake up and realize that the one to whom they have trusted their lives as shepherd is a deceiver and a destroyer, they would run to Jesus for salvation and refuge.

Authority Over Powers

In Luke 10:19, Jesus declared, "I have given you authority to trample on snakes and scorpions and to overcome all the power of the enemy; nothing will harm you." This Scripture should be memorized and appropriated by every believer. It is your authority to believe that you are completely and absolutely free from the power of the Devil. Once you are born again, you have nothing to fear from the Devil. He is the one who is actually fearful.

Luke 10:17 tells us that the seventy disciples whom Jesus sent out to preach returned with much joy. They said, "Lord, even the demons submit to us in your name." Jesus then tells them why this was so. He replied, "I saw Satan fall like lightning from heaven" (Luke 10:18). Satan is fallen, like Babylon of old. He has fallen from power. His hold over Christians has been broken. Any time a person becomes a Christian he is no longer under the jurisdiction of Satan's power. He is now free and authorized to even cast Devils out of other people and out of nasty situations. It is your right as a child of God. But great as this is, we should not rejoice in this possibility, but rather "because your names are written in heaven" (v. 20). Our salvation is our most valuable asset and should be the cause of our rejoicing, and not any miracles we may do in His name.

The Greek New Testament brings out our authority over Satan more vividly. The words translated power in English are two different words in the Greek. The verse should actually read: "Behold, I give you authority (exousia) to tread on serpents and scorpions, and over all the power (dunamis-dynamic, dynamite) of the enemy. The Christian is like a traffic policeman who can bring traffic to a halt with the wave of his hand. He uses his authority over the power of the motor vehicles. It would be futile if he tried to control traffic with brute force, and potentially very dangerous. So is it with the Christian. We are not told to fight the Devil on our own, but with the power of God. Satan is already defeated by the cross. When Jesus said, "It is finished" on the cross, that spelt the end of Satan's rule.

Satan exhausted his sting on Jesus at Calvary. At the resurrection his doom was signed and sealed. "Where, O death, is your victory? Where, O death, is your sting?" (1 Corinthians 15:55) "No, in all these things we are more than conquerors through Him who loved us" (Rom 8:37). There is no need to fight a defeated enemy. The Devil is defeated. For the Christian, the Devil is only a roaring lion. He makes a lot of noise and roars, but he has lost the power to bite.

The Power of a Praying Christian

The authority we have over the Devil has been given to us by Jesus Christ Himself. It is not received through some secret initiation ceremony or formula. Christ has given us authority over demons because everything He did on the cross, in the grave, and at the resurrection was for us. He had no sin to die for. His death on the cross was for our sins. He had no need to be delivered from Satanic oppression. His resurrection victory was for us. "And having disarmed the powers and authorities, he made a public spectacle of them, triumphing over them by the cross" (Colossians 2:15). Jesus openly paraded His victory over Satan so that we may have confidence in His total and complete victory over him. You need not fear the Devil because Jesus has defeated him. He is totally powerless over the Christian who knows his rights in Christ. Your victory has been secured on the cross.

The promise of victory is for you. Don't let the Devil make you think it is meant for everyone else but you. It is for you, my beloved. God had you in mind when He made this promise. But as with every promise of God, you must have faith that God means what He says and expect Him to act on your behalf. Hear Him say it, "Behold, I give YOU power (authority)." Believe it; act upon it. It's for you.

You Have the Authority to Put the Devil in his Place

The authority we have is to tread on serpents and scorpions. These are agents of the Devil, demonic powers and forces of evil. They are already under our feet. Now tread on them! There is nothing to fear. "Nothing shall by any means hurt you." There is nothing the Devil fears more than a Christian on his knees before God. The picture we have of the Devil in the New Testament is that of forces who know their end is near. They cower and tremble at the command of Jesus.

In the synagogue when Jesus was casting out Devils, they came out of the people crying and screaming because they knew their doom had come. Some spoke through their victims and begged Jesus not to cast them out into the open. "We know who you are, the Son of God. Have you come to torment us before the time?" Jesus did not engage in conversation with them, because they were unclean creatures. He cast them out with a word.

Don't be afraid to speak to Devils and cast them out in Jesus' name. There is no arguing with them. Some people pray to God to deal with the Devils. That may be a noble thing to do, but our Lord Jesus wants us to deal with them directly ourselves, using the authority He has given to us through His name.

2. AUTHORITY over a DEFEATED ENEMY

J esus says, "You shall know the truth, and the truth shall make you free" (John 8:32). Knowing the truth of who you are in Christ is of utmost importance in taking our stand against the powers of darkness. The Bible says, "If any man be in Christ, he is a new creation, old things are passed away; behold, all things are become new" (2 Corinthians 5:17). We have been changed. We are new. We are no longer under the authority of Satan. We are now under the authority of Christ. God has "...raised us up together and made us sit together in heavenly places in Christ Jesus" (Ephesians 2:6). Satan will therefore fight tooth and nail to keep the Christian from knowing his right in Christ. For those who know their standing in Christ, he will try to prevent them from using their authority.

The Devil's Smokescreens

Firstly, he puts up a smokescreen by pretending he is not active in a particular situation, trying to convince us it's all natural or circumstantial. People give all sorts of names to problems which are really the work of devils and should be seen as having spiritual roots and dealt with accordingly. However, if you walk in the flesh, in the natural, and not in the Spirit, Satan can hide in people, in circumstances, in diseases, etc. Then everything under the sun can get the blame for his works.

Secondly, by bluffing his way through ignorance of God's Word. He tells people (even through some preachers) that the authority over demons is no longer available to us today; or at best, that it is the reserved solely for a few giants of faith. His master stroke is to cause a smokescreen. When Christians command devils to leave a person or a place or a situation, they sometimes go quietly and will not manifest. This gives the impression they are not the ones responsible for the mayhem and distress. The one praying may come to the conclusion that either he was mistaken in his diagnosis, or perhaps they were present and had not run away.

God is a good God, and the Devil is a bad Devil. More often than not the Devil is the one behind all bad things. A Christian who knows how to deal with them will not give up until good times return. Life sometimes can be like the cat and mouse game Pharaoh was playing with Moses. He would give some concessions to allow the Israelites to leave Egypt, and then renege, or say they should go without their cattle, or without their children. However, Moses did not settle for anything less than total evacuation. Use your authority to get total victory over every area of your life. Nothing should be under demonic control; not your health, your business, your family, or your ministry. Nothing!

No Need to Struggle

The way to fight the Devil is not by rolling up your sleeves and preparing for a power struggle with him. It is not by hurling loud abuses at him or calling him horrible names. In a sinister way he loves that. He wants people to take notice of him and constantly talk about the ways he is tormenting them.

One famous American pastor, who had been successful in the ministry of deliverance had the shock of his life. It came after one of his well-attended deliverance services when the Holy Spirit warned him about his giving undue respect to the Devil in his church. It was his practice to bind the powers of Satan at the start of Sunday worship, and to cast them out of the auditorium.

The Holy Spirit, however, told him that his church had become a favorite haunt of demons. Of all places, the pastor reasoned, demons should be terrified of coming near our church. This is where we get them expelled from people. However, the Holy Spirit showed this man of God that hordes of demon spirits came to his church just to be worshipped and didn't mind being cast out later. "Incredible!" thought the preacher. "How can demon spirits come to my church to be worshipped?" The Holy Spirit insisted they did and told him how.

On the last Saturday of the month the pastor held a deliverance service on the church premises. People came from all over the area to witness the miracles and receive their own breakthroughs. Sundays after the pastor felt it necessary to cleanse the building of any spirit still loitering. He did this by asking the congregation to bow their heads in prayer. Then he would proceed to bind the spirits in the building and cast them out.

As far as the evil spirits were concerned, the members of the congregation were closing their eyes and bowing their heads to them. That's what they came back for: reverence from the believers. Once they got what they came for they did not mind what the pastor did to them. This pattern was repeated every first Sunday of the month.

The pastor had learnt a big lesson from this revelation. From that time on, the pastor was determined to start every service with praise to the Lord instead of focusing on the enemy. Whenever he wanted to deal with evil spirits, he would never ask his congregation to close their eyes or bow their heads. When you are dealing with the Lord, deal with the Lord; and when you are dealing with the Devil, deal with the Devil. But do not mix the two exercises.

Don't ignore the Devil, as if he is irrelevant in our everyday life. And neither should you pay him and his hordes too much attention. Jesus did not ignore them. Throughout his ministry he dealt firmly with demonic powers. But he did not argue with them or hold long conversation with them. Some ministers go overboard in displaying demonic activities, playing videos and audio recordings of deliverance sessions, particularly the more demonstrative ones. Jesus, on the other hand, did not permit them to hold center stage or speak too long.

Stand Your Ground

One of the most effective ways to fight the Devil is to stand your ground. "Finally, be strong in the Lord and in his mighty power. Put on the full armor of God, so that you can take your stand against the Devil's schemes. For our struggle is not against flesh and blood, but against the rulers, against the authorities, against the powers of this dark world and against the spiritual forces of evil in the heavenly realms. Therefore, put on the full armor of God, so that when the day of evil comes, you may be able to stand your ground, and after you

THE AUTHORITY OF THE BELIEVER

have done everything, to stand" (Ephesians 6:10-13). Paul says, "We are not ignorant of the wiles of the Devil." One of his wiles, or schemes, is to lure a Christian out of his position of safety and security in Christ. He makes him feel like the fight is between the two of them, whereas it isn't. In a way, there is no fight at all. The Devil is already defeated. Jesus has conquered him on the cross once and for all. We don't need to fight a defeated enemy. What we do is to stand our ground, claiming our redemption rights. It is a fight of faith: faith to claim what Jesus has secured for us by His death and resurrection.

The Fight of Faith

The fight of faith begins by knowing your position in Christ and taking your stand on that truth. "The truth shall set you free." By knowing your position in Christ, you will be able to "Be strong in the Lord, and in the power of His might." This means that the Lord's strength has become your strength, and his power is at your disposal.

The Psalmist said, "The Lord is always at my side, I shall not be moved." You stay right in the Lord, knowing that your position in Christ is secure, and that "nothing shall by any means hurt you." This will take care of the enemy's attack on your inner security. Now we must face his attacks on our outer defenses. For that, we "take the whole armor of God." This is where the enemy attacks the mind of the Christian with thoughts of unworthiness, weakness, and a sense of inferiority to stand in the presence of God. He may even remind the Christian of his past sins and failings; sins which have been confessed and have been forgiven.

As the Devil attacks with thoughts of fear, worry and anxiety, you put up the shield of faith. As he attacks with thoughts of defeat and depression, you resist him by claiming the promises of God.

Praise God, I Spilled the Orange Juice

George Verwer, the leader of Operation Mobilization (a ministry that sends young people around the world preaching the gospel) related this experience in one of his talks. One hot summer he led a gospel mission to Europe. Young people from many countries in Europe and America had travelled to France to distribute gospel literature. Many of these young people were living on a shoestring, as they didn't have spare cash. The entire mission was based on living by faith, and so luxury items were out of the question.

It was a very hot summer in France, and they had nothing but water to quench their thirst. Then, out of the blue, a kind-hearted farmer gave the team several baskets of oranges. This was definitely a luxury item. Everybody witnessed the delivery of the oranges and looked forward to refreshing drinks of orange juice with their evening meal.

Some of the girls came back to the camp early to squeeze the juice into a big vat ready for the evening treat. Evening came and everybody returned for the prayer meeting before the evening meal. It was a lively prayer meeting, helped partly, I dare say, by the thought of downing their meal with refreshing, cool orange juice!

George Verwer had to leave the prayer tent early for another engagement. He quietly walked out through an adjoining tent, the dinning tent, where the vat full of orange juice was kept. And it was dark in there. He stumbled and kicked something heavy. When his eyes got accustomed to the darkness, helped by a glimmer of light from outside, it all became clear that he had just kicked the orange juice container. A whole afternoon's labor of love and the special treat all the hard-working young people were looking forward to was gone. He had spilled the lot. He felt awful. He could have kicked himself. How was he to explain to the people in the prayer meeting? Summer crusades were quite demanding, trekking from one village to another, trying to witness for Christ in a language you could hardly speak. Then coming back to a very basic campsite with no comfort was asking a lot. Common orange juice was quite a treat under those circumstances.

It seemed like the Devil stood between him and the prayer tent, taunting him. He felt depressed and disappointed in himself. How would he face the people? What could he say to them? Then he realized the Devil was trying to take advantage of the dire strait. He was the one behind his feeling of guilt and depression. Immediately he put up his shield of faith and shouted at the top of his voice to the crowd in the tent: "Hallelujah! I've just spilled the orange juice."

First, there was dead silence. Then the whole place was filled with rumbling of suppressed laughter, as everyone got the victory over their disappointment. They turned it into a praise meeting after that. The Devil lost and Jesus won. It could, however, have ended quite differently, had George Verwer not used his shield of faith against the subtle attack of the enemy.

3. WHAT we are IN CHRIST

When Jesus hung on the cross, he said, "It is finished." That means the work of our redemption is finished. There is nothing for us to do towards our salvation. It is all paid for. Praise God for that. The moment a person believes in Jesus as Lord and Savior, he enters into a new life, a new privilege, a new blessing. The Bible says, "Therefore, if anyone is in Christ, the new creation has come: The old has gone, the new is here!" (2 Corinthians 5:17). He is a new creation. All a Christian now needs to do is know the meaning of this new creation. Once he knows it, he need only to believe it and live in the freedom of it. There is nothing more to do. It is finished.

If you ever wonder what God thinks of you as a Christian, listen to this: You have been made the righteousness of God in Christ. "God made Him who had no sin to be sin for us, so that in Him we might become the righteousness of God" (2 Corinthians 5:21). When God sees you, he sees you in right standing with Himself. The blood of Jesus has cleansed all your sins. You stand before God whole and complete, without any guilt or blame. You are accepted in Christ. "To the praise of his glorious grace, which he has freely given us in the One he loves" (Ephesians 1:6).

God is on your side: no one can judge you or condemn you. "What, then, shall we say in response to these things? If God is for us, who can be against us? He who did not spare his own Son, but gave Him up for us all—how will he not also, along with Him, graciously give us all things? Who will bring any charge against those whom God has chosen? It is God who justifies" (Romans 8:31-33). "He did it to demonstrate his righteousness at the present time, so as to be just and the one who justifies those who have faith in Jesus" (Rom 3:26).

You stand before God justified. Not just forgiven; it is far more important than that. When God justifies a person, he restores him back to the position Adam lost. It is as if he had never sinned or belonged to Adam's lost race. God doesn't see you as a forgiven sinner cowering in his presence or as an unworthy soul who is not allowed to claim any privileges. At the Garden Tomb after Jesus had risen from the grave, he said to Mary Magdalene: "Jesus said, "Do not hold on to me, for I have not yet ascended to the Father. Go instead to my brothers and tell them, 'I am ascending to my Father and your Father, to my God and your God." (John 20:17). The Father of our Lord Jesus Christ is now our Father also. He loves us as much as He loves Jesus. "I in them and you in me—so that they may be brought to complete unity. Then the world will know that you sent me and have loved them even as you have loved me. (John 17:23) His love for us was so great that He sent His only Son to die in our place. We are the apples of His eyes. You don't need to feel inferior in the presence of the Lord because He sees you justified in Christ, just as if you never fell with Adam. It is a complete and total restoration. If God is on your side, who can stand against you? Nobody, in heaven, on earth, or under the earth.

You are in heavenly places with Christ, now. "And God raised us up with Christ and seated us with Him in the heavenly realms in Christ Jesus" (Ephesians 2:6).

When Jesus rose from the dead and ascended into heaven, we were in Him. We took part in His victory. Legally, we are seated with Him in heavenly places where sitting is a position of rest and authority. We are reigning with Him. Praise God! Once you get the vision of the position of the believer in Christ, you will look at life from a different level. This is why the Devil is under our feet: we are above him in Christ, who is the head of all things.

You are complete in Christ. "For in Christ all the fullness of the Deity lives in bodily form, 10 and in Christ you have been brought to fullness. He is the head over every power and authority" (Colossians 2:9,10). Legally you lack nothing. You are complete in Christ. All the blessing you will ever need, all the provisions you will ever want, all the power you will ever seek are yours in Christ. If you can grasp this truth and walk in it, how tremendous! A lot of Christians are constantly begging God in prayer to do for them what He has already done for them in Christ. They are the man in James who looked into the mirror and immediately forgot his own image. "Do not merely listen to the word, and so deceive yourselves. Do what it says. Anyone who listens to the word but does not do what it says is like someone who looks at his face in a mirror and, after looking at himself, goes away and immediately forgets what he looks like" (James 1:22-24).

One way to act on the word of God is to make sure your confession—the words you speak—both in prayer and in general conversation, agree with the word of God. Wrong confession can rob you of your redemption rights in Christ, so that you continue to struggle for what is already yours.

You are light in the Lord. "You are the light of the world. A town built on a hill cannot be hidden. In the same way, let your light shine before others, that they may see your good deeds and glorify your Father in heaven" (Matthew 5:14, 16). We Christians are so identified with Christ that we are actually called the light of the world. He is called "the true light that lights everyman that comes into the world" (John 1:9). This means that he lives in us and expresses his light and life through us. As He is, so are we in the world. As the darkness cannot overcome Him, so no power of darkness can overcome us. Any attempt by the Devil to pull dark clouds of doubt, fear or depression over a Christian is just a smokescreen. He is bluffing. Resist him in the name of Jesus Christ, and he will flee.

A member of a religious cult came to the house of one of our church members one day and brought a warning. He told her to pray hard, for he had seen a vision of her car involved in some accident. Although she couldn't see how God would reveal a true vision to an unsaved person, she decided to pray about the prediction anyway; just to be on the safe side. However, the enemy already had got his foot in the door. She believed the false prophet enough to pray about his prediction. Fear had let Satan in.

About a month later her brand-new car burst into flames. It wasn't even running. So, she began to wonder why God allowed it to happen. About six months later the same 'prophet' re-appeared at her house. He commiserated with her over the loss of her car. He had heard through the grapevine what took place. He reminded her that had she accepted his previous offer to go on a special session and fasting on her behalf, the disaster could have been averted.

Unfortunately, he had more bad news to deliver. This time around the troubles brewing in the not-too-distant future were on her personally and would last several years unless she puts a stop to it. Like before, his remedy was simple and easy. He would step into the gap for her in prayer and fasting with secret formulae that would get the enemies off her back. It would cost her, of course, as he would give her case his total attention.

She wanted to dismiss this latest prophecy, but because the first one had apparently come true, she was puzzled. "How can an unsaved soothsayer prophecy an event and it happens; and why would God allow bad things to happen to His children?" she reasoned. It was at this point she came to me with these questions. My advice was to take no notice of the man. It is an old trick of the Devil. Firstly, he makes a wild guess of a future event, so as to cause fear and panic, then he uses that doorway of fear to enter the person's life. Then he causes the event he had predicted. I advised her not to even mention the latest prophecy in prayer. Just ignore Satan and he will go away. She did, and never had any more bother.

Safe in the Arms of Jesus

The Devil cannot predict your future if you are a true child of God. The Bible gives us assurance about that. It says, "For you are dead and your life is hid with Christ in God" (Colossians 3:3). Satan cannot reach where we really are: with Christ in God. You and I, my Christian brother and sister, are hid inside God. Isn't that wonderful? Any pretense that Satan makes at knowing your future is just a bluff. He knows the past only too well, especially before we were saved, because he had his hand in it. The past is now under the blood of Jesus.

Isaiah 41:22-24 tells us about the inability of the gods of the heathens to tell the future. "Tell us, you idols, what is going to happen. Tell us what the former things were, so that we may consider them and know their final outcome. Or declare to us the things to come, tell us what the future holds, so we may know that you are gods. Do something, whether good or bad, so that we will be dismayed and filled with fear. But you are less than nothing and your works are utterly worthless; whoever chooses you is detestable." Only God, our heavenly Father, has the secret of our future in His hands. For three and a half years God hid His prophet Elijah from the wicked king Ahab, and none of his four hundred and fifty Baal prophets could reveal where God was hiding His servant. Surely, if Satan knows the secrets of the Lord, he would have revealed where Elijah was hiding to the starving king. In no way can darkness overcome light.

When Paul was warning the Christians at Corinth against the danger of being unequally yoked with unbelievers, he said, "Do not be yoked together with unbelievers. For what do righteousness and wickedness have in common? Or what fellowship can light have with darkness?" (2 Corinthians 6:14). You are light if you have put your trust in the Lord as your Savior. These are your privileges in Christ: they are yours by right of adoption.

Christ in You

"Out of his fullness we have all received grace in place of grace already given" (John 1:16). All who have trusted in

Christ for their salvation have received as part of their inheritance the fullness of Christ. All his power, riches, glory and authority he has bestowed on us. In the Old Testament God says, "I am the Lord; that is my name! I will not yield my glory to another or my praise to idols" (Isaiah 42:8). However, in the New Testament, where believers have come into the fullness of Christ, Jesus prayed in John 17:22, "I have given them the glory that you gave me, that they may be one as we are one." Isn't Jesus wonderful to share his glory with us, we who used to be "dead in trespasses and sins"? To God be the glory!

How do you feel now? With all these privileges and blessings, is it not thinkable that Satan should have any power over you? "To them God has chosen to make known among the Gentiles the glorious riches of this mystery, which is Christ in you, the hope of glory" (Colossians 1:27). Remember that not only has Christ saved you from your sin, but he also lives in you. "You, dear children, are from God and have overcome them, because the one who is in you is greater than the one who is in the world" (1 John 4:4). These are promises to be claimed by faith. These are redemption realities. This is what you are in Christ. This is how God sees you, and the Devil knows it. Now you must see yourself as Christ sees you, and as he tells you in his Word. Don't be like the man who looks at himself in the mirror, and goes away, and "straightaway forgets what manner of man he was."

If only more Christians would walk in the light of what they are in Christ, they would have less of a problem with faith. Jesus never worried about faith. He didn't need to because he knew who he was. He is the Son of God, and all things have been delivered unto Him. He knew it and lived in it. You, too, should do the same. Memorize these Scriptures which tell you what you are in Christ; meditate on them until they sink into your heart and accept yourself as God sees you. This is your confidence in your stand against the wiles, attacks and attempts of the Devil to draw you out of your secure position into the open for a fight. "So do not throw away your confidence; it will be richly rewarded" (Hebrews 10:35).

Once you begin to live in the light of your position in Christ, your confidence becomes second nature. The Devil will testify before you, too, saying "Jesus I know, Paul I know." He won't then say, "but who are you?" because he will know that you know who you are: his master in Jesus' name.

4. STUNTED LIVES

If this is the truth of our position in Christ, someone might well ask, "Why aren't all Christians living in victory?" A good question. The Bible is the Word of God, and what it says about us is true. The problem with many of us is that we simply don't know our rights in Christ. When reading our Bibles, we just gloss over the truth revealed to us about our position in Christ. We fail to apply the Word to ourselves personally. We may see it as Paul writing to the Corinthians, the Ephesians or the Philippians; but not to us. Some read the Scriptures as if they are all in the future, promises that must be grasped at in prayer with concentrated effort.

Many Christians are living in spiritual bondage, and they don't even know it. It is possible to have lived so long in a state of spiritual limitation that one comes to accept it as the norm. The Devil has managed to put a ceiling on the life of many Christians so that they do not enjoy the full benefit of their privileged position in Christ. They accept defeat, despair, depression, and a lack of spiritual power as a way of life.

Have you ever wondered why so many Christians who claim to be baptized in the Holy Spirit—even speak in tongues—still live powerless, mediocre lives? Ideally, once a person is filled with the Holy Spirit, he should have no problem living a victorious life, utilizing the power of God. For the Bible says, "But you will receive power when the Holy Spirit comes on you; and you will be my witnesses in Jerusalem, and in all Judea and Samaria, and to the ends of the earth" (Acts 1:8).

There is no other source of power apart from the Holy Spirit. Power does not come by prayer and fasting. It is not through preaching or shouting at the top of your voice. Power is in the Holy Spirit who lives in the believer. "It is "Not by might, nor by power, by My Spirit, says the Lord of hosts." (Zechariah 4:6) What then hinders this power of the Holy Spirit within Christians from flowing out freely to bless the world? Why does the Devil ignore the command of so many when they rebuke him, and try to cast him out?

The answers are manifold, but surely one of them is that many Christians allow the Devil to take up too much room in their lives. Consequently, the enemy has put a ceiling on their lives. This may have taken place before their conversion and carried forward into their Christian experience, so that they expect nothing higher.

A scientist researched the behavior of body lice. He put a louse in a glass jar in his laboratory, and then put a lid on the jar. Throughout the day the scientist observed the louse leaping up trying to escape, but his head kept hitting the lid. The following day the scientist removed the lid. Throughout the day he observed the louse continued to leap to the top of the jar. Then fall back down to the bottom. Even though the lid had been removed, the louse would not leap higher than where the lid was on the first day. This louse had become conditioned to having a lid on his life!

Isn't this similar to what the Devil does to a lot of Christians? Through lack of confidence in who they are in Christ, and through spiritual bondage brought forward from unconverted days, the Devil puts a false ceiling on their lives.

5. BINDING and LOOSING

When I was praying for the baptism of the Holy Spirit soon after I became a Christian, I had high hopes of having the power to do the works Jesus says those who believe on Him would do. Jesus says, "Very truly I tell you, whoever believes in me will do the works I have been doing, and they will do even greater things than these, because I am going to the Father." (John14:12). I believed what the Bible says here, and I knew fully well that the promise was for every believer. It is for "He that believes on me"," and I believed on Him. I knew also that this ability to do the works that Jesus did would come when I received the baptism of the Holy Spirit. For the Bible says again:

> "Whoever believes in me, as Scripture has said, rivers of living water will flow from within them." By this he meant the Spirit, whom those who believed in Him were later to receive. Up to that time the Spirit had not been given, since Jesus had not yet been glorified. (John 7:38, 39).

The Holy Spirit was not given until Jesus was glorified at the right hand of the Father in heaven after the ascension. So, I had it all worked out that if I could only receive the baptism of the Holy Spirit, I too would receive the power Jesus promised. Then one glorious day I received this baptism of the Holy Spirit and spoke in tongues. It was a wonderful experience, which I shall never forget. I felt the power of God tingling through my entire body. Months went back and I began to wonder what had happened to the power I expected.

Although I had a greater liberty in prayer and worship I had not known before, I didn't have the success I expected when dealing with demonic powers. When I cast demons out my words seem to bounce back at me. I was disappointed. I sought more power through hours of prayer and fasting, but with little success. Two and a half years later I got my answer. The problem was not in getting more power, but finding out what was hindering the power from flowing out fully and freely.

I tried to cast Devils out of other people when I was in fact allowing them room in my own life. Until I understood that I needed deliverance, my attempts at spiritual warfare were like pouring water into a basket. I was getting nowhere fast. Although I didn't know that I had brought spiritual bondage from my past. I was involved in occult practices and wearing of charms and amulets as a non-Christian. To protect myself from some evil forces I had taken refuge with other spirits, exchanging one form of bondage for another.

Unaware, these demonic forces followed me into my Christian life, sapping away my spiritual power in the Lord. But someone might ask, "Are Christians not free from these demons the moment they believe on Jesus?" Yes, and no! If a new Christian really understands the part these forces play in his pre-conversion days, and he also fully understands the meaning of a believer's baptism, he can be delivered at baptism. At baptism a believer is buried with Christ and raised with Him (Colossians 2:12). He goes down into the water in burial symbolically and comes out of the water in resurrection life.

He is dead to the past. The Devil has no claim on him. He is free from the guilt of sin at conversion, and free from demonic bondage at baptism. Even after the initial deliverance every Christian should be vigilant and make sure that he does not leave room for Devils to get a foothold into his life and home.

Once I understood my position, I quickly sought for a spiritual leader to pray for me, and I was delivered. From that time, I've had no trouble dealing with Devils. They have to obey me in the name of Jesus.

6. SPIRITUAL ADULTERY

Dabbling with occult powers and spiritism is a form of spiritual adultery. When a person is joined to the Lord, he is one spirit with Him, and when he deals with evil spirits, he becomes one with those spirits. The Bible says, "Do you not know that he who unites himself with a prostitute is one with her in body? For it is said, 'The two will become one flesh.' But whoever is united with the Lord is one with Him in spirit." (1 Corinthians 6:16, 17) God wants his children to be pure in every way, in body and in spirit. "You were bought at a price. Therefore, honor God with your bodies."

God hates spiritual adultery and did not permit it among his people, Israel. "When you enter the land the Lord your God is giving you, do not learn to imitate the detestable ways of the nations there. Let no one be found among you who sacrifices their son or daughter in the fire, who practices divination or sorcery, interprets omens, engages in witchcraft, or casts spells, or who is a medium or spiritist or who consults the dead. Anyone who does these things is detestable to the Lord; because of these same detestable practices the Lord your God will drive out those nations before you." (Deuteronomy 18:9-12)

Spiritual Contaminations

Among spiritual contaminations common today are:

1. Palmistry: divination from the palm of the hand. Fortune tellers read the lines on a person's hand to tell past events in the life.

2. Spiritism: communication with the dead, trying to gain information from a departed relative, etc. This could be as innocent-looking as talking to the picture of a departed father or husband. Some people speak to corpses just before burial, telling them what they will do to look after their children, etc. Any attempt to talk to the dead presents an opportunity for evil spirits to enter into a relationship with that person. It can be very dangerous.

3. Ouija Board: a board with letters of the alphabet and a figure that turns round pointing at various letters in turn to spell out a message, or answers questions.

4. Cutting the flesh: small lacerations are made on the wrist, the side, the forehead, chest, etc., and a fetish potion rubbed into them. "Do not cut your bodies for the dead or put tattoo marks on yourselves. I am the Lord." (Lev.19:28).

5. Horoscope: daily reading of the star under the various signs of the Zodiac. When a star crosses the path of another star people whose stars are affected are not supposed to make friends on that day, or alternatively they are encouraged to make friends on that day as their stars favor it. This mild form of spiritism has come to be accepted as the norm in many homes. Horoscopes are now found in many newspapers and periodicals.

6. Talisman: this includes magical rings, amulets, waist bands. They are supposed to provide protection, neutralize spiritual attacks, and generally bring good luck.

It is not always the person involved who is responsible for contacting the spirits. Sometimes concerned parents take their children to pagan festivals and dedicate them to some gods for protection. A very sick child may be taken to a fetish priest for a cure, and the child gets involved with spirits that way. Some children inherit spiritual problems from grandparents three generations back.

A family that had lots of mental illness and psychiatry disorder in the children was found to have a great-grandmother who was a spiritualist medium. Sometimes people whose parents had charge of idol shrines have been known to possess psychic powers. Women in pagan societies who go to idols for children can have children who are possessed with spirits at birth. These are familiar spirits which appear to the child as friendly "little people". Only the possessed child can see these "friends." Grown-ups can also allow these spirits to enter them through certain rites. Those who have confessed and been delivered tell horrifying tales of wickedness they effect in the power of these spirits.

In some cases, however, a person may be possessed without being an active participant in the wicked works of these spirits. He or she may not see them, but he is subjected to bizarre and wicked dreams. These dreams can be so vivid they appear like real life. They eat, sleep, travel, marry and have children in them. One tell-tale sign is that on waking the body feels heavy, as if something is pressing it down on the bed.

As soon as one girl became a Christian, her dreams changed. The 'friends' turned on her. Night after night in her dreams an old man would chase her around with intent to endanger her life. She would wake up exhausted as if she had been running all night. She tried to call the name of Jesus in her dreams, but no sound came out. I prayed for her to be delivered. That night she was able to shout the name of Jesus at the old man. He disappeared from her dreams, and she had no more trouble with bad dreams again. After she was delivered her spiritual life was revolutionized. A few days later she was baptized in the Holy Spirit. She began to pray aloud in public worship, something she couldn't bring herself to do before.

Now this brings me to the question people often ask: Can a Christian be demon possessed?

7. CHRISTIANS and DEMON POSSESSION

C an a Christian be demon possessed? This is a vexed question among Christians today. Some believe the Devil cannot enter a Christian, while others maintain it is possible for a Christian to come under some form of demonic power. Christian experience around the world has shown that it is possible, and indeed it is widespread, for Christians to be under the influence of demons. This is possible where people had dabbled in the occult before their conversion or allowed Satan to enter them through some incidents in their lives. For example, natural fear can turn into a spirit of fear if the Christian gives too much room in his life to fear.

There is no way truly born-again Christian can be demon possessed, but demons can enter a Christian to carry on their activities. When a person is born again, the Holy Spirit begins to live in him. He becomes the temple of the Holy Spirit, and the Holy Spirit will never share the same room with a demon. However, demons can manifest themselves through the person's soul and body. They can cause fear, worry, anxiety, depression, bad thoughts, unbelief, and sloth. Have you ever noticed how some people are quite lively and alert during all parts of a service until it's time for the message? It is then they can't keep their eyes open for drowsiness.

The Devil cannot possess a Christian, but he can oppress, depress, afflict, torment or tempt. These are some of the remedies:

Resist the Devil

"Resist the Devil, and he will flee from you" (James 4:7) "Be alert and of sober mind. Your enemy the Devil prowls around like a roaring lion looking for someone to devour. Resist him, standing firm in the faith, because you know that the family of believers throughout the world is undergoing the same kind of sufferings." (1 Peter 5:8, 9).

Be Delivered

Go to a church leader with experience in spiritual warfare for a prayer of deliverance. "Deliver us from evil." (Matthew 6:13) "The Lord will rescue me from every evil attack and will bring me safely to his heavenly kingdom. To Him be glory for ever and ever. Amen "And the Lord will deliver me from every evil work." (2 Timothy 4:18) "Since the children have flesh and blood, he too shared in their humanity so that by his death he might break the power of him who holds the power of death—that is, the Devil—and free those who all their lives were held in slavery by their fear of death." (Hebrews 2:14, 15)

Cast Them Out

"And these signs shall follow them that believe; in my name shall they cast out Devils" (Mark 16:17). "Heal the sick, cleanse the lepers, raise the dead, cast out Devils: freely you have received, freely give" (Matthew 10:8).

Be Set Free

"You shall know the truth, and the truth shall make you free."

(John 8:32) "It is for freedom that Christ has set us free. Stand firm, then, and do not let yourselves be burdened again by a yoke of slavery." (Galatians 5:1)

Know Your Position in Christ

"The God of peace will soon crush Satan under your feet. The grace of our Lord Jesus be with you." (Romans 16:20) "I have given you authority to trample on snakes and scorpions and to overcome all the power of the enemy; nothing will harm you." (Luke 10:19) "You shall tread upon the lion and the adder: the young lion and the dragon you shall trample under foot." (Psalm 91:13) "Put on the full armor of God, so that you can take your stand against the Devil's schemes." (Ephesians 6:11)

Wield Your Authority Over Him

"Then he called his twelve disciples together, and gave them power and authority over all Devils, and to cure diseases" (Luke 9:1). "The Lord will grant that the enemies who rise up against you will be defeated before you. They will come at you from one direction but flee from you in seven." (Deuteronomy 28:7)

These are the weapons of our warfare. "The weapons we fight with are not the weapons of the world. On the contrary, they have divine power to demolish strongholds" (2 Corinthians 10:4). Use them!

8. THE ENEMY at the BACK DOOR

I t is essential to know the area where the enemy works, his methods and tactics, so that one does not fight as one beating the air. If you don't believe that the Devil can work in the life of a Christian, then you've allowed him his first victory, for he loves to hide behind ignorance. The Devil has a field day with people who deny his existence or choose to ignore his activities. The apostle Paul says that we are ignorant of his devices.

If you have a persistent problem that just will not go away, even after much prayer, ask the Lord to show you if the Devil is behind it. If it is, then ask Him to show you what kind of spirit is involved. If you think you can deal with it by yourself. Be firm and be specific. Tell the Devil, calling it by name, to leave you immediately. Do not hesitate or feel intimidated. Just use the authority Jesus has given you. If, on the other hand, you don't feel up to it, get a spiritual leader to pray for you.

Some Ways Satan Can Affect Christians

"But Peter said, Ananias, why has Satan filled your heart to lie to the Holy Spirit, and keep back part of the price of the land?" (Acts 5:3) This dreadful misdemeanor was carried out by born again Christians. While the Holy Spirit was working in a mighty revival, Satan had the chance to slip a lie into the hearts of this couple. They should have resisted him, but they didn't, perhaps they didn't believe the Devil could work in

Christians. See what the SCRIPTUREs says, "Satan filled their heart to lie."

The apostle Paul had to deliver a believer to Satan for the destruction of the body. "So, when you are assembled and I am with you in spirit, and the power of our Lord Jesus is present, hand this man over to Satan for the destruction of the flesh, so that his spirit may be saved on the day of the Lord." (1 Corinthians 5:4, 5)

After repeatedly turning a deaf ear to exhortations to repent from fornication, this born-again Christian in Corinth was handed over to Satan. He was still a saved Christian, but he must have died prematurely, unless he repented. Paul had to perform this unpleasant task again to safeguard the purity of the church. "Holding faith, and a good conscience, which some having put away concerning the faith have made shipwreck: of whom is Hymenaeus and Alexander, whom I have delivered unto Satan that they may learn not to blaspheme." (1 Timothy 1:20)

There is no doubt that Paul was dealing with Christians here. He says in his letter to the Corinthians that he only judged those "that are within." "What business is it of mine to judge those outside the church? Are you not to judge those inside? God will judge those outside. Expel the wicked person from among you." (1 Corinthians 5:12, 13) These are extreme cases, but they show that Satan can affect Christians if they are not vigilant. If you are aware of this then there is no danger of you living in a world of make believe, where ignorance is bliss.

Thank God for the victory we have in Jesus, but no one can enjoy this victory unless he is made aware of the possibility that Satan can slip in through the back door of his life. He can come in through sin, bad habits, moral lapses, and lack of watchfulness.

Spirit of Buffeting

"Because of these surpassingly great revelations. Therefore, in order to keep me from becoming conceited, I was given a thorn in my flesh, a messenger of Satan, to torment me." (2 Corinthians 12:7) Clearly the apostle Paul knew that the problem and difficulties he was having (the persecutions, beatings, shipwrecks, and imprisonments that dogged his life) were far beyond the call of duty. He knew that an agent of Satan was behind it all. If these spirits can't get inside, they will surround the believer, trying to trip him up. Since they are operating from outside you can't really cast them out. One must pray to God, sometimes with fasting, and ask Him to "deliver us this day from evil (the evil one)."

In the case of Paul, however, God had a higher purpose. He was using these spirits to keep his servant in spiritual trim. Paul said, "Three times I pleaded with the Lord to take it away from me. But he said to me, 'My grace is sufficient for you, for my power is made perfect in weakness.' Therefore, I will boast all the more gladly about my weaknesses, so that Christ's power may rest on me." (2 Corinthians 12:8, 9) The table had been turned on Satan. The very problems he intended to depress and discourage Paul, God used to strengthen his servant. So much that Paul actually looked forward to these infirmities.

I have yet to see a strong, mature Christian who has not had to pass through hard times. A good athlete must use weights to develop his muscles, making him fit and strong. All of us have from birth the same number of muscle fibers. As we grow up, we allow these muscles to develop normally. We can neglect exercises and let them go fat and flabby, or we can, if we are enthusiastic, apply extra pressures on them and develop super muscles rippling with health and vitality.

Christians should welcome problems and difficulties. I don't mean we should go out of our way looking for trouble or have a persecution complex when we expect nothing but trouble all our lives. But if problems come, we should not allow them to overpower us. Every problem can be a doorway to a prospect.

Heaven is for overcomers, not for weaklings who are just waiting for death or the second coming of Christ, so that they can escape this wicked world. It is not designed for people who want to bypass life, tiptoeing along the edges. Heaven is for people who "Know their God, and are strong, and do exploits." (Daniel 11:32) People who will look at impossibilities and say, "It shall be done."

The Bible says, "In all these things we are more than conquerors." What can the Devil do, what can anybody do? The Bible says, "Fear not them which kill the body, but are not liable to kill the soul" (Matthew 10:28). Nobody can take your joy away; they can't take Jesus away from you. Paul says that to be absent from the body and present with Christ is far better. Death holds no terror for committed Christians. Praise the Lord!

A pastor went through a time of financial hardship. His salary, which had been sufficient, suddenly became inadequate, though his circumstances hadn't changed. Month after month he found himself unable to meet his financial commitments, bills piled up. If the car didn't give trouble, it would be something in the house requiring repairs. Months followed months without any improvement. Then the Lord showed him that the Devil had a hand in his finances. He promptly resisted the Devil and told him to get his hand off his money. His finances went back to normal. But in the meantime, he had learned a great lesson in trusting God in a difficult situation.

Hindrances

"For we wanted to come to you—certainly I, Paul, did, again and again—but Satan blocked our way." (1 Thessalonians 2:18) There are many ways Satan can try to hinder God's people, and God's work. He can cause people to be at loggerheads with each other, bringing disunity and misunderstanding. He can cause poverty, so that God's people just don't have the means to carry out His work.
A lethargic spirit can come over people so that they don't feel like doing anything for the Lord.

The Devil can come into a life through some childhood experience. We had to pray for a young married woman, who had been sexually assaulted by her stepfather when she was only eight. She grew up depressed and had difficulties getting along with men. For no reason apparent to her she just didn't like men. This was affecting her relationship with her husband. We felt she had an unclean spirit inside her, and after prayer she was delivered.

Not everyone in need expresses obvious signs of oppression. Once the Spirit of God starts to move in a place or a meeting these spirits can be forced to manifest themselves. They may lie dormant in a person, not manifesting themselves until an anointed servant of God challenges them to reveal themselves. The problem could be as serious as a spirit actually speaking with the voice of the person concerned, down to a mild form of bondage of not being free to worship the Lord with hand clapping, raising the hands up in praise, and extolling God with shouts of Hallelujah.

9. BE THOU MADE WHOLE

I t is important that we deal with spiritual contaminations that afflict Christians, so that the way may be clear for you to exercise your rights in Christ and use your authority to deal with the forces of Satan. If you have had any dealings with the occult, such as I mentioned in a previous chapter, then you need deliverance. You can usually pray for yourself, but if you feel you are not getting anywhere it will be wise to get a spiritual Christian to pray for you. It is essential that you are free from all forms of bondage before praying for other people or situations that demand deliverance. If not, the Devil may just ignore you. You can't cast him out of others if you allow him room in your own life. Yu must be made whole.

You can pray a prayer like this:

"Lord Jesus, thank you for saving me and setting me free. I ask you to forgive me for dabbling with the powers of darkness (name them). Please, cleanse me, and cover me now with your precious blood. Thank you for hearing my prayer."

Then open your eyes and direct these next words to the Devil. "In the name of Jesus, I come against you, Devil. I bind your power over my life. Right now, I cut myself off from my past dealings with you. I stand on redemption ground and plead the blood of Jesus over you. Leave me right now in Jesus' name."

Then you can worship and praise the Lord for setting you free. I have prayed for hundreds of people in this way, and the results have been the same every time: complete victory. I have seen people's lives transformed almost over-night after prayer for deliverance.

If you have ever been involved in the occult, but nevertheless feel some sort of spiritual bondage, powerlessness, or inability to fully enter into true worship and praise, use the word of God. By confessing the word of God, and claiming his promises, you will experience a new release and freedom in your spirit. You must believe that what you say will happen. "Truly I tell you, if anyone says to this mountain, 'Go, throw yourself into the sea,' and does not doubt in their heart but believes that what they say will happen, it will be done for them." (Mark 11:23)

Confession of the word of God always precedes possession. Confession is more than telling God how bad you are. It has a positive side. It means to agree with God about what he says you are. You may not feel what you are saying in agreement with the word of God, but if you persist and don't lose your confidence in the word of God, your confession will become a reality.

The Bible says, "We walk by faith, and not by sight." (2 Corinthians 5:7) Don't allow your five senses to dominate you and dictate to you what you believe. To a lot of people what their senses tell them carries more weight than what the word of God tells them. For instance, on healing, you pray for some people, laying hands on them according to the word of God, and they go away disappointed, saying they can still feel the pain.

A lady I once prayed for refused to believe she was healed, because she still felt pain. She said, "I won't tell a lie. I can't say I'm healed when I'm not. I can still feel the pain." This lady actually thought she was being honest and realistic. Whereas she was in fact full of unbelief. The Bible says, "They shall lay hands on the sick, and they shall recover." But her senses told her she still had pain. She then decided to believe what her senses told her, and set aside what the Bible tells her, that she is healed.

No one can receive anything from the Lord without faith. In fact, it is impossible to receive anything from God without faith. And faith is nothing more than believing that what God says in his word is true (in spite of the evidence of the senses). It isn't that we should no longer trust our senses or tell lies about our symptoms. You don't say you have no pain when it is still there. But you don't confess it either. You ignore your feelings and confess the word of God instead. Then your confession brings possession.

This is the way to enjoy your deliverance. Once you've prayed, or you've been prayed for, believe that you are free, confess that you are free. You may or may not feel any immediate change, but you confess the word of God. "Resist the Devil and he will flee from you." You have resisted the Devil, and according to the word of God, he has fled.

10. CONFESSION Brings POSSESSION

As you confess the word of God, you begin to possess what it says. When you speak out God's word, he is honor-bound to confirm it. He says, "So is my word that goes out from my mouth: It will not return to me empty but will accomplish what I desire and achieve the purpose for which I sent it." (Isaiah 55:11) God has declared that his word will never return to him void. This means that it will not return to him without making good what it states. God wants you to speak his word back to him, and when you do so in faith, that word will return to him, not empty but fulfilled. Don't confess defeat and doubt, but confess the word of God in faith.

"Then the Lord said to me, "You have seen well, for I am watching over my word to perform it." (Jeremiah 1:12) Another translation has it: "I am behind my word to perform it". "He shall have whatsoever he says." (Mark 11:23) "We also believe, and therefore speak." (2 Corinthians 4:13)

You Are What You Confess

"The words of the reckless pierce like swords, but the tongue of the wise brings healing." (Proverbs 12:18) By confessing God's promises on healing you can bring divine health to your body. "Death and life are in the power of the tongue." (Proverbs 18:12) You can do yourself a lot of harm if you constantly confess negative things. How the Devil is tormenting you, or what a hard time you are having in life. Rather you should confess God's word, that it may change your situation, and bring life and blessing your way. "The tongue of the wise adorns knowledge, but the mouth of the fool gushes folly." (Proverbs 15:2) Use your knowledge of the word of God to overcome the enemy and live in victory, health, and spiritual power.

When we were in America, my wife and I met a lady, the wife of a Senator, and a lovely Christian. Because of some infection in her womb, she had to have an operation to remove a section of it. Medically speaking she could no longer have a baby, and her doctor told her so. But she refused to believe it. Instead, she kept on believing the word of God which says that none shall be barren in the land. Daily she would place her hands on her womb area and bless it in the name of Jesus, and she would claim the promises of God. A couple of years or so after her operation she began to feel a lump in her womb. At first she ignored it. When it got bigger, she went for a medical check-up. Her doctor was puzzled, but deduced it might be the tumor he had cut off was flaring up again. The lady, however, insisted she was pregnant. The doctor, of course, laughed it off because it was impossible. The fallopian tube had been cut off. But the lady was right. She was pregnant. Faith in the promises of God had brought the impossible. She delivered twins.

The Faith of Abraham

Have faith like Abraham, who "Against all hope, Abraham in hope believed and so became the father of many nations, just as it had been said to him, 'So shall your offspring be.' Without weakening in his faith, he faced the fact that his body was as good as dead—since he was about a hundred years old—and that Sarah's womb was also dead. Yet he did not waver through unbelief regarding the promise of God, but was strengthened in his faith and gave glory to God." (Romans 4:18-20)

When God promised Abraham a son with Sarah, their situation could not have been more hopeless. He was about 100 years old, and she was about 90, well past childbearing age. In the natural they could not have children, but God had spoken, and his word will always be fulfilled. Abraham ignored what his senses were telling him and concentrated on what the word of God told him. He exchanged sense knowledge for revelation knowledge. His senses told him his body was as good as dead, as well as Sarah's womb. The word of God, on the other hand, revelation knowledge, told him, "I have made you a father of many nations." (Romans 4:17)

What did Abraham do about the word of God? He was "being fully persuaded that God had power to do what he had promised." (Romans 4:21) So he gave glory to God (v.20). He spent the time between the promise and the proof (when Isaac was conceived) confessing God's word and giving glory to Him.

Someone asked Martin Luther, "Do you feel that you have been forgiven?" He answered, "No, but I'm as sure as there is a God in heaven, for feelings come and feelings go, and feelings are deceiving; my warrant is the word of God, naught else is worth believing." "Though all my heart should feel condemned for want of one's sweet token, there is one greater than my heart whose word cannot be broken. I'll trust his unchanging love, till soul and body sever; For though all else shall pass away, his word shall stand forever."

11. THE OVERCOMING LIFE

T hey triumphed over him by the blood of the Lamb and by the word of their testimony; they did not love their lives so much as to shrink from death." (Revelation 12:11) In whatever circumstances you may find yourself, always recognize the fact that you are standing on redemption ground. That means you are covered in the blood of Jesus. Satan cannot touch you, for the blood of Jesus sealed his defeat.

You should make a habit of daily confessing the word of God. This may be in prayer or in a whisper as you go about your work. Someone has said, "A confession a day keeps the Devil away." Get into the routine of saying the right things, for your words play an important part in your life. Confession of faith plays an important part in the overcoming life. As confession always precedes possession, so a wrong confession precedes the possession of wrong things. The moment you say you have no faith, fear will grip you. If you say, "I think I'm catching a cold," it is amazing how quickly the cold begins to overpower you and get worse. You don't have to confess negative things. You can say, "I am catching a healing" when a cold is coming on. You don't have to live on your senses all the time.

Paul says, "I can do all this through Him who gives me strength." (Philippians 4:13) I am quite sure there were many things Paul couldn't do in his own strength, but he didn't confess that; he confessed his new creation position in Christ. So should we.

Jesus said, "For by your words you will be justified, and by your words you will be condemned." (Matthew 12:37) No one is ever saved until they confess Jesus as Lord. You must say with your mouth what your heart believes. Romans 10:9 says, "If you declare with your mouth, 'Jesus is Lord,' and believe in your heart that God raised Him from the dead, you will be saved." Confession always precedes possession. It is when you confess that you believe that Jesus has come into your heart, that you will experience the assurance of salvation. If you confess negative things, needs, weakness, sickness, fear, it means that is what you really believe in your heart. "For out of the abundance of the heart the mouth speaks". It is what is inside that will come out. So why don't you fill your heart with the right things: the word of God. The Bible says, "Let the message of Christ dwell among you richly as you teach and admonish one another with all wisdom through psalms, hymns, and songs from the Spirit, singing to God with gratitude in your hearts." (Colossians 3:16)

The Confession of Faith

Don't say you are bound and find it difficult to express what you feel, but confess that "If the Son, therefore, shall set you free. You shall be free indeed." (John 8:36) Don't say you find it difficult to love people, but confess that "Hope does not put us to shame, because God's love has been poured out into our hearts through the Holy Spirit, who has been given to us." (Romans 5:5)

If you feel shy and timid, confess that "the righteous are bold as a lion" (Proverbs 28:1), and possess boldness in spiritual warfare. If you feel lonely and despondent, remember to declare: "Keep your lives free from the love of money and be content with what you have, because God has said, 'Never will I leave you; never will I forsake you.' So we say with confidence, 'The Lord is my helper; I will not be afraid What can mere mortals do to me?'" (Hebrews 13:5, 6)

The Scripture shows us how to use the word of God. It says that because the Lord has said something, we should then boldly declare it: to make the promise ours in experience. The Lord has promised to be with you, and never to leave you. Jesus is as close as the mention of his name. "The Lord is near unto all them that call upon Him, to all that call upon His name in truth." (Psalm 145:18) There is no need for a Christian to be afraid of the dark, thunderstorms, or accidents. Jesus is with you everywhere you go. Nothing comes your way without passing through his nail-pierced hands. If someone who is bigger and stronger than you threatens you, you need have no fear. You declare: "I will not fear what man shall do unto me." Because the Lord is your helper, this is your confession. Don't go around seeking sympathy by telling people what the enemy is doing to you, and what a hard time you are having. Sing hymns and psalms and spiritual songs in your heart to the Lord. The Lord is with you.

A missionary to Nigeria was stopped at gunpoint and robbed of his car. Then one of the thieves aimed his pistol to shoot him, so that he could not identify them. But the missionary told the thieves they could not shoot him. He knew Jesus was with him and trusted him to defend him and his family.

When the thief pulled the trigger, his gun jammed. In desperation they drove off.

Later the missionary and his family got a lift to the police station and reported the theft. The police asked if he could identify the men. "Describe?" he said, I'll do more than describe, I'll draw their picture." The missionary happened to be a good artist. The police recognized the ringleader immediately, and that night arrested the gang, and recovered the car. Has Jesus not said, "I will never forsake you"? "Behold, they shall surely gather together, but not by me: whosoever shall gather together shall fall for your sake. No weapon that is formed against you shall prosper; and every tongue that shall rise against you in judgment you shall condemn. This is the heritage of the servants of the Lord, and their righteousness is of me, says the Lord." (Isaiah 54:15, 17)

You don't need to be afraid of anybody or anything. There is no power on earth or in hell that can harm a child of God. Satan couldn't touch Job because God had put a hedge round him. But we have a surer protection in the New Covenant. "Your life is hid with Christ in God." (Colossians 3:3) This does not mean we shall never suffer persecution or have problems. We will have our fair share of problems and disappointments, but only such as God permits for the fulfilment of his purpose in our lives. In it all we come out on top. Don't be afraid for the Lord says to you, "So do not fear, for I am with you; do not be dismayed, for I am your God. I will strengthen you and help you; I will uphold you with my righteous right hand." (Isaiah 41:10)

Fear is not of God; it is of the Devil. Fear need have no part in your heart, because God had promised to help you, strengthen you, and always be with you. The Lord says, "Fear not: for I have redeemed you, I have called you by my name; you are Mine." (Isaiah 43:1) You are redeemed by the blood of Jesus, therefore Satan, the author of fear, has no power over you. "Greater is he that is within you, than he that is in the world." (1 John 4:4)

12. GET OFF the DEVIL'S PRAYER LIST

One of the ways a mature Christian can fall into the snare of the Devil is by praying the wrong kind of prayer. It is as if Satan has a long list of prayer items; he looks for zealous Christians who want to be their best for God. He says, "Do you like praying? Here is a long list for you". By giving them the wrong information, he keeps them busy going round in spiritual circles, so that they make little or no progress. It is an old trick of the Devil. He tried it on Adam and Eve in the Garden. He got them to believe they were naked and should be ashamed of themselves. Once they had eaten the forbidden fruit, their eyes were opened, they were ashamed and sewed fig leaves together to cover themselves, and then the couple went about seeking for solution to that need.

God said to Adam, "who told you that you are naked? Have you eaten of the tree that I commanded you not to eat?" (Genesis 3:11) Yes, who told Adam that he was naked? God didn't. His knowledge of his need did not come through revelation knowledge from the word of God. He got it from the Devil. Adam had begun to live in the flesh, and not in the Spirit. When you live in the Spirit only what the Bible says is important. Revelation knowledge supersedes sense knowledge. What God tells you in his word becomes your eyes, nose, ears, and mouth. If what your sense tells you about yourself contradicts what the Bible says about you, believe the word of God, and ignore your senses. This is what Abraham did in the face of the promise of God. "He considered not his own body now dead, when he was about a hundred years old." (Romans 4:19) When God promised to give him a son by his wife Sarah, both of them had long passed the childbearing age. Abraham ignored this sense knowledge, "He considered not his own body now dead; neither yet the deadness of Sarah's womb". Instead, he was "fully persuaded that what he (God) had promised, he was able also to perform."

The Devil would have had Abraham barking up the wrong tree by concentrating his prayers on the deadness of his own body, and the barrenness of Sarah's womb. "Abe, I know God tells you you'll have a son by Sarah, but you are both past the age. Why not pray for rejuvenation?" But God didn't tell Abraham he and his wife needed rejuvenating. He said, "Sarah your wife shall bear you a son indeed; and you shall call his name Isaac." (Genesis 17:19)

It was this promise that Abraham concentrated on, not his own body. "Yet he did not waver through unbelief regarding the promise of God, but was strengthened in his faith and gave glory to God." (Romans 4:20) A lot of Christians don't have the faith of Abraham; they follow the example of Adam instead. Adam sewed fig leaves to cover a nakedness God didn't tell him about. When in disobedience he ate the fruit, the glory of God, which had previously covered him, became invisible. Adam now saw himself as he was in the natural, not as he was in the Spirit, so he went about trying to cover up.
We need to see ourselves with two kinds of eyes: the natural and the spiritual. Our spiritual eye gets its information from the word of God. If the Devil tells you to take a closer look at yourself with the natural eye and see what an awful state you are in spiritually, wait a minute before you start to pray along

the lines the Devil is suggesting. Of course, you won't know initially that it is the Devil giving you such ideas.

If you know in your life, much is to be desired, then get on your knees and let the Holy Spirit show you areas where you may need to confess and forsake your sins. But don't let the Devil bring you under condemnation and lead you to a life of legalism. He will want you to cry and weep all the time over your sins. Each time you look at yourself you will see nothing but bad things. This way you will lose your joy and freedom in the Spirit. You will become engrossed in your efforts to get perfect. And the Devil will make sure you never run out of things that need putting right.

Instead, look into the word of God, and confess what it says about you. Remember you are a new creation. The way to grow in grace is not to try to pray the old man out of existence, but by allowing the Holy Spirit to work out in you the new man which is already in you. The Bible says that Christ is in you. The way to grow is to stop trying to perfect through self-effort (which is as bad as trying to get saved by your own works), and let Christ live out his life through you. It is a state of perfect rest.

Many years ago, I used to spend up to six hours a day on my knees praying that God would make me perfect. I wanted to be holy. But with all my praying I would cry unto the Lord, telling Him to change me from a sinful, weak Christian. Then one day he rebuked me for praying such words of unbelief. He showed me that I was still living in the past. Who told me I was sinful and weak? God didn't. He tells me in his word I have been redeemed, I am the righteousness of God in Christ Jesus, old things are passed away, I've been blessed with all spiritual blessings in the heavenly places in Christ, and that the Lord is my strength.

Once my eyes were opened to what I really was in Christ, I got off the Devil's prayer list, and started thanking God for what I am in Christ. I didn't feel any different immediately, but within a short while I began to notice a marked difference in my life. The word of God had produced its fruit in my life.

Counteracting the Devil's Suggestions

The Devil says, "You know you find it hard to love people." The Bible says, "Hope does not put us to shame, because God's love has been poured out into our hearts through the Holy Spirit, who has been given to us." (Romans 5:5) It is God's will that you should be "rooted and grounded in love" and "might be filled with all the fullness of God (who is love)." (Ephesians 3:17, 19) "For the Spirit God gave us does not make us timid, but gives us power, love and self-discipline." (2 Timothy 1:7) You don't have to be praying to God to fill your heart with love, when his word tells you that you have received the spirit of love. You have received it, it's all yours. So why pray for what is yours? The Holy Spirit has already spread the love of God in your heart. Search no further. You only need to thank God for what he has given you, in spite of your feelings to the contrary. Give Him the glory.

Satan would want you to pray harder for love, and for power, and for success, etc., as if you are an impoverished soul that needs more blessing from God in order to become better and more successful. This is not Bible faith. There is no love, power, or success outside of Christ. Christ is life: He is love. Not that Christ has love, and if you can persuade Him with tears, He will give you more love, so you can love better. He is love. God is love. If you want love, ask Jesus in. Once He is inside your heart, you have love. You now need to have fellowship with Him, allow the Spirit to show you what might be hindering his love from flowing freely, and you'll be amazed at the results.

The Devil says, "You will fail that exam. You will fail to get that promotion. You will fail to keep that new friend. You know you never seem to succeed in anything important." God's word says, "But thanks be to God, who always leads us as captives in Christ's triumphal procession and uses us to spread the aroma of the knowledge of Him everywhere." (2 Corinthians 2:14) You don't have to pray frantically for success in life, in your job or in your relationship with people. Expect success and prosperity, because God's word says, "Dear friend, I pray that you may enjoy good health and that all may go well with you, even as your soul is getting along well." (3 John 2) "No one will be able to stand against you all the days of your life. As I was with Moses, so I will be with you; I will never leave you nor forsake you." (Joshua 1:5) "That person is like a tree planted by streams of water, which yields its fruit in season and whose leaf does not wither - whatever they do prospers." (Psalm 1:3)

So, when you feel like praying for success, remember what God says about you and how he sees you. He says you are "blessed with all spiritual blessings in heavenly places in Christ." (Ephesians 1:3) "I will give you every place where you set your foot, as I promised Moses." (Joshua 1:3) These Scriptures are for you. Thank the Lord for making you a success in whatever you do. As you face that exam, that promotion prospect, that friendship, that new career, tell the

Lord in prayer that you are confident he will cause you to succeed, because he has promised to give you every place that the sole of your foot shall tread upon.

Jesus didn't fail. He said, "It is finished." He finished the work his Father gave Him to do. "I have finished the work which you gave me to do." (John 17:4) Paul did not fail either. He said, "I have fought the fight, I have kept the faith, I have finished my course." If they succeeded, so can you. Paul testified, "For God, who was at work in Peter as an apostle to the circumcised, was also at work in me as an apostle to the Gentiles." (Galatians 2:8) The same God is mighty in you, too. The Devil says you can't do anything for God because you are weak, so you pray for strength. God says you are strong, and you can do anything through Christ, who is your strength. (Philippians 4:13) "That is why, for Christ's sake, I delight in weaknesses, in insults, in hardships, in persecutions, in difficulties. For when I am weak, then I am strong." (2 Corinthians 12:10) "Let the weak say, 'I am strong'." (Joel 3:10) You are not weak, because God says you are strong. He has promised to strengthen you and uphold you with his right hand of righteousness. (Isaiah 41:10) In prayer claim the help and strength he has promised you. Don't confess your weakness and inability to do things.

The Devil will want you to pray for acceptance before God, saying that your sins have separated between you and God, and make you feel inferior in God's presence. Don't fall for that trap by praying to be accepted in God's sight, or to be a better Christian. The work is already done. "He predestined us for adoption to sonship through Jesus Christ, in accordance with his pleasure and will—to the praise of his glorious grace, which he has freely given us in the One he loves." (Ephesians 1:5, 6)

"Therefore, brothers and sisters, since we have confidence to enter the Most Holy Place by the blood of Jesus, by a new and living way opened for us through the curtain, that is, his body, and since we have a great priest over the house of God, let us draw near to God with a sincere heart and with the full assurance that faith brings, having our hearts sprinkled to cleanse us from a guilty conscience and having our bodies washed with pure water." (Hebrews 10:19-22)

There is an open invitation for you into the presence of your heavenly Father. There is no need to feel inadequate or inferior in his presence. You don't have to weep and wail before Him to make your voice to be heard or confess your unworthiness. Come boldly into His presence and draw near in full assurance of faith. God wants you to come into his presence as a son not as a beggar. All the treasures of heaven are at your disposal. You are "heirs of God and joint heirs with Christ." (Romans 8:17)

13. WRESTLING with PRINCIPALITIES

P ut on the full armor of God, so that you can take your stand against the Devil's schemes. For our struggle is not against flesh and blood, but against the rulers, against the authorities, against the powers of this dark world and against the spiritual forces of evil in the heavenly realms. (Ephesians 6:11, 12) As there are hierarchies in the kingdom of God, such as cherubim, seraphim, and angels, and archangels (like Michael and Gabriel), so there are hierarchies in the kingdom of Satan. These are the principalities, powers, rulers of the darkness of this world, and spiritual wickedness in high places.

The spiritual wickedness in high places are evil spirits that can cause affliction, depression and oppression. They cause bad habits inspire lies, cause deafness, blindness, dumbness, and sometimes crippling diseases. Their main target is the body of men and women. It would seem that they prefer to express themselves through humans. Outside human bodies they are elastic bands under tension, stretched to the limit. It is only when they find someone, some creature, or somewhere to express themselves that they can feel at home. "When an impure spirit comes out of a person, it goes through arid places seeking rest and does not find it. Then it says, 'I will return to the house I left.' When it arrives, it finds the house unoccupied, swept clean and put in order." (Matthew 12:43, 44)

These spirits take whoever or whatsoever they inhabit as their rightful home. Consequently, they don't like to be told to leave, and will not do so unless the Christian is authoritative and refuses to tolerate their activity. Evil spirits are often responsible for diseases and malfunctions in people. Doctors talk about germs, bacteria and tumors as causes of many ailments, but germs and other micro-organisms that cause diseases are often energized by demon spirits. As the body without the spirit is dead, so these living organisms cannot harm anyone without demon spirits. This is why Jesus sometimes cast demons out to heal certain diseases. "While they were going out, a man who was demon-possessed and could not talk was brought to Jesus. And when the demon was driven out, the man who had been mute spoke. The crowd was amazed and said, "Nothing like this has ever been seen in Israel." (Matthew 9:32, 33) When the spirits are cast out, the germs or bacteria die, and the patient begins to recover, and the normal process of healing takes over.

The hierarchies in the kingdom of Satan, the principalities, etc., tend more often to work without possessing people. They work in big organizations and involve themselves in activities of national governments. They plan and execute catastrophe, famine, wars, violence, and inspired world cults. Their main aim is to prepare the world for the coming of the antichrist when they hope to establish Satanic rule on earth.

The Christian Warfare Against Fallen Angels

When Satan fell from heaven because of sin, he took a third of the angels with him. No doubt he must have promised them power and independence and told them that they would be makers of their destiny. He tricked them just as he tricked Eve. Many angels left their first estate and followed him, not knowing that defeat and eternal doom would result. However, Satan would not have embarked on such a rebellion against God if he didn't believe he could succeed. He still believes that he can win, but he has shifted his attention to men. If he can't win the throne of God in heaven, where he said, "I will be like the Most High," (Isaiah 14:14) he will battle for God's throne in the hearts of men.

Satan will fail again, for he has not reckoned with God's plan of redemption. Not everyone will bow the knee to Baal. There are countless number of people from every tongue, tribe and nation who are redeemed by the blood of the Lamb, "They triumphed over him by the blood of the Lamb and by the word of their testimony; they did not love their lives so much as to shrink from death." (Revelation 12:11)

Satan's original plan was to secure the defection of the majority of the angels. He would be in a position to easily overwhelm those who might remain loyal to God. Here again he failed, for the majority were faithful, and Michael and his angels ejected Satan and the disobedient angels from heaven. The Devil isn't going to have it easy here on earth either, for God has raised up a new breed of warriors, the born-again Christians, you and I, who are blood-washed Children of God. Satan has now to contend with an innumerable number of angels in the heavens, and a mighty host of Spirit-filled Christians, who love nothing more than God, and fear nothing but sin. God is allowing the Devil freedom to work and to do his worst in the world for the time being. In his vain hope the Devil thinks given the chance all men would follow the self-centered way that he had chosen.

"Does Job fear God for nothing?" Satan replied. "Have you not put a hedge around him and his household and everything he has? You have blessed the work of his hands, so that his flocks and herds are spread throughout the land. But now stretch out your hand and strike everything he has, and he will surely curse you to your face." (Job 1:9, 11) He was wrong about Job then, for "In all this, Job did not sin by charging God with wrongdoing." (Job 1:22) He is wrong about Christians today, too. Christians the world over in every generation know that their archenemy is the Devil. No Spirit-filled Christian would allow Satan around causing havoc and destruction in lives and nations unchallenged. He is doomed! He himself knows that he is fighting a losing battle, but as the end time draws to a close, he becomes more desperate and seeks to drag as many people as possible down to hell with him.

Angels and Men United in Warfare

The defection of Satan and his angels left a gap in heaven. God, however, had seen all this ahead of time, and made plans to replace Lucifer and his fallen angels by a race of men and women, "With flattery he will corrupt those who have violated the covenant, but the people who know their God will firmly resist him." (Daniel 11:32) As Adam had dominion over Eden at one time (Ezekiel 28:13), so the new race of Christians have been given dominion over the renewed creation.

In Daniel 10:12, 13, we see the conflict between the angels of God and those loyal to Satan. While Daniel was praying with fasting, the messenger from heaven sent to give him God's answer was resisted by the prince of Persia. This is the demonic prince over the kingdom of Persia where the people of God were held in captivity. Daniel's persistence in prayer and fasting for 21 days gave strength to the angel, who eventually received reinforcement from Michael, the archangel. We are not alone in our wrestling against the forces of evil, the angels are fighting with us. (Psalm 34:7)

There are other instances in the Bible where angels came to the rescue of godly men in their stand against the forces of evil. Elisha was not alone in the struggle against the enemies of Israel. When the armies of Syria surrounded the city of Dothan to capture Elisha, the invisible armies of the Lord were behind him. "Don't be afraid," the prophet answered. "'Those who are with us are more than those who are with them.' And Elisha prayed, 'Open his eyes, Lord, so that he may see.' Then the Lord opened the servant's eyes, and he looked and saw the hills full of horses and chariots of fire all around Elisha." (2 Kings 6:16, 17) We don't read that Elisha prayed for special protection, only that he prayed that the Lord might open the eyes of his servant Gehezi to see the angelic hosts around them. When you are fighting for the Lord, you don't have to pray to make God know his responsibility toward you. Jesus says, "Your heavenly Father knows what you have need of before you ask Him." His angels surround those who fear Him—who live in holiness and soberness and walk in the Spirit—and are always ready for battle.

Take the Battle to the Gates

The Christian's conflict with the powers of darkness is not a defensive one. God expects, and indeed has equipped us, to take the battle to the gates of the enemy camp. "And I tell you that you are Peter, and on this rock I will build my church, and the gates of Hades will not overcome it." (Matthew 16:18) A lot of people see this verse backwards. They see the church as having the gates, for defense and protection, and the forces of evil battering them, but unable to overpower them. Actually, it is the Devil who needs protection against the onslaught of the Church. We are to take the battle to Satan, right up to his door; and he will not be able to withstand our attack.

You are a very important person in the kingdom of God, and Satan knows it. The Bible says, "And from Jesus Christ, who is the faithful witness, the firstborn from the dead, and the ruler of the kings of the earth. To Him who loves us and has freed us from our sins by his blood and has made us to be a kingdom and priests to serve his God and Father—to Him be glory and power for ever and ever! Amen." (Revelation 1:5, 6) "You have made them to be a kingdom and priests to serve our God, and they will reign on the earth." (Rev 5:10) "As God's co-workers we urge you not to receive God's grace in vain." (2 Corinthians 6:1)

An American giant of a man, who had a grudge against all preachers, went on a rampage one night. He had already broken the jaws of one preacher, when he charged into a large tent meeting where a famous preacher was speaking. As he strode toward the platform, arms raised in anger, the police moved in to restrain him. The preacher, however, told them to leave the man alone. Just as he raised his strong, powerful fist to bring down the fateful blow, the preacher commanded, "Devil, come out of him, in Jesus' Name." Immediately his arm went limp like jelly and he slumped on the ground, weeping like a child. He confessed that he hadn't meant to do anybody any harm, but there was something inside him pushing him. The preacher knew this and used his authority in Christ.

14. THE CHRISTIAN ARMOR

As we wrestle with the powers of darkness and use our God-given authority over the Devil, we must bear in mind that he fights like a drowning man. He knows that he is doomed to defeat, but he fights on to see how many he can take down with him. It is sad how many good Christians have been caught in his web.

Paul says we should not be ignorant of Satan's devices. Satan is crafty and cunning. He is a master of trickery and deception. While we must exercise our authority over him, we must not lose our respect for him. It isn't that we are afraid of him, but we do not play with fire. Some people pride themselves in their ability to cast Devils out, and go about it in a most crude, if not dangerous, manner. They hurl abusive words at the Devil, calling him offensive names. Some preachers even hold long conversations with demons before commanding them to come out. They may think they are being clever, but it is not really the Biblical way. While they play around, the Devil is busy looking for ways to trip them up.

A dreadful thing happened to a one-time world-famous evangelist, who used to deal with demons with frivolity. He ended a life of powerful ministry a drunk. This man became careless and allowed the Devil to trip him up.

We Are All in the Battle

Christians do not decide whether or not to enter the conflict with the principalities and powers. Once you are born again by the Spirit of God, you enter the battle between Christ and Satan. We are not here as onlookers. There is a war on, and, whether we like it or not, we must fight on one side or the other of the battleline. Indeed, one way to end up in defeat is to presume it is not your fight and play dead on the battlefield. Paul tells us in Ephesians 6 that "We wrestle not against flesh and blood, but against principalities and powers." There is no choice in the matter.

In the early church, many Christians had to defend their faith in the arena wrestling with wild beasts. Paul is saying that in the real battle of life the Christian wrestling is not with people or beasts, but with spiritual forces. Therefore, we must have the appropriate spiritual armor for defensive and offensive actions.

Our Loins Girt with Truth

Paul, in describing a typical Roman soldier's armor, saw the leather girdle around the waist as being of utmost importance. To facilitate ease of movement, the toga was made of leather strips. These were held together by a thong tied around the waist like a belt. This way the soldier could move freely, and yet the belt holding the pleats ensures that the overlapping strips leave no gap.

The Christian is to hold his armor together with truth. Nothing has done more damage to the church of Jesus Christ than false doctrines. These errors have led many a good and godly person into spiritual darkness and moral decay. It is essential that we be protected with the truth of the word of God.

The Breastplate of Righteousness

We meet the Devil with righteousness, not our own but Christ's righteousness imputed to us. Having been washed in the blood of Jesus, we stand before God as if we have never sinned. Hallelujah! The Devil may come with lies that we are not worthy to claim certain promises or enjoy certain blessings in Christ. We claim the righteousness of Christ, which God has imparted to us. We are righteous, not because of our works, but by his grace.

The Gospel of Peace

Sharing our faith is part of the armor. As you preach the gospel, or simply talk to someone about the Lord, sharing your experience, the Bible says you will get adequate protection for your feet. The feet speak of walking. The Christian walk becomes smoother, safer, and more fulfilling when we witness to our faith. A witnessing Christian is a growing Christian!

The Shield of Faith

The Devil's quiver is full of poisonous darts: worry, anxiety, fear, inferiority complex, depression, oppression, discouragement, unbelief, bad thoughts, pain. As he shoots these darts, the shield of faith bounces them off. If he brings fear, you reject it because God says, "You have not received the spirit of fear." (2 Timothy 1:3)

The Helmet of Salvation

We have a wonderful salvation in Christ; it's full and free. But the enemy can strike a blow on our head, so that we begin to live in the flesh and not in the Spirit. As the head is the center of our nervous system, containing eyes, nose, ears, and mouth, so we need to protect our spiritual perception and sensitivity.

The Sword of the Spirit

The sword of the Spirit, which is the word of God, refers to the rhema, the anointed spoken word of God. It is this word of faith, that accomplishes the work of God. We take the offensive against Satan with the word of God and the anointing of the Spirit, which destroys the yoke.

15. PRAYER and FASTING

When Jesus saw that a crowd was running to the scene, he rebuked the impure spirit. "You deaf and mute spirit," he said, "I command you, come out of him and never enter him again." The spirit shrieked, convulsed him violently and came out. The boy looked so much like a corpse that many said, "He's dead." But Jesus took him by the hand and lifted him to his feet, and he stood up. After Jesus had gone indoors, his disciples asked him privately, "Why couldn't we drive it out?" He replied, "This kind can come out only by prayer and fasting." (Mark 9:25-29)

The preparation of the person casting out demons is as important as his knowledge of his authority over the powers of darkness. Nothing will happen in the spiritual warfare unless the believer is adequately prepared. That preparation includes prayer and fasting.

A missionary lady was confronted with a demon-possessed man, who the church couldn't help. They had prayed for several days for this man, with no visible result. Face to face with this challenge the missionary felt inadequate, not knowing what she could do to help the man, when the whole church had failed. She decided to go into fasting for three days. At the end of her fast she felt an overwhelming sense of spiritual authority, and the anointing of the Holy Spirit. She went over to the room where the man was kept under observation and commanded the spirit to leave him. There was a loud crashing noise. The spirit had left the man and escaped through the window, shattering the glass. The man was completely healed. Although most spirits would come out at a word of command there are some stubborn ones which will not leave without a fight. The disciples came across such a spirit, when a desperate man brought his son possessed of a dumb spirit to them. No doubt they were full of confidence since they had never failed to get results before. It came as a shock when this particular spirit proved stubborn and refused to come out. The puzzled disciples asked Jesus why they could not cast it out.

The Lord did not upbraid them for lack of faith but showed them the additional preparation necessary for an effective ministry of deliverance. There are certain demons that cannot be cast out except by those who are fully equipped to deal with them. Prayer and fasting here does not mean that you must spend all your time on your knees and spend days and days fasting until you are emaciated. Rather it means the time spent by the earnest Christian preparing his soul in readiness for any need that may arise.

There is a well-known preacher, whose ministry God has blessed over the years, who made a habit of spending two or three weeks alone with the Lord in Prayer and fasting, about twice a year. Some Christians keep themselves disciplined by fasting for one day every week. Fasting is an intensive form of prayer. It is also a way of praying without ceasing. The fasting prayer is the deepest way you can express your heart's desire to God. There is no better way one can really tell God how desperately he wants something.

Whenever some people in the Bible were in deep trouble, they turned to prayer and fasting to make their voice heard on high. "There, by the Ahava Canal, I proclaimed a fast, so that we might humble ourselves before our God and ask Him for a safe journey for us and our children, with all our possessions. I was ashamed to ask the king for soldiers and horsemen to protect us from enemies on the road, because we had told the king, "The gracious hand of our God is on everyone who looks to Him, but his great anger is against all who forsake Him." (Ezra 8:21, 22)

The passage through a no-man's land swarming with highway robbers, with no protection for the children and the valuables, demanded not only a strong faith, but the assurance that God was with them. That was why Ezra proclaimed a fast. Whenever men wanted assurance of God's presence and power, they always added fasting to their prayers. When Paul and his companions were caught in a terrible storm on their way to Rome, he proclaimed a fast, which lasted fourteen days. At the end an angel of the Lord appeared to Paul to give him the assurance of God's hand on the ship.

"Last night an angel of the God to whom I belong and whom I serve stood beside me and said, 'Do not be afraid, Paul. You must stand trial before Caesar; and God has graciously given you the lives of all who sail with you.' So keep up your courage, men, for I have faith in God that it will happen just as he told me." (Acts 27:23- 25) After the fast, Paul had received God's assurance of blessing and a terrible disaster was averted.

Fasting is a way of releasing our spirit. Very often the soul and the body completely over-shadow the spirit, so that it cannot express itself. In fasting, when the body is denied its natural craving for food, the spirit comes into its ascendancy. It is a well-known fact that unbelief is banished through fasting, and there is an increased sense of the presence of God.

The fasting Christian finds it easier to believe God for miracles. Such spiritual power is released through fasting that demon spirits cannot stand before it. If you want to be a successful Christian worker, someone whose prayers are answered, and to have demons obey your command, live the fasted life. Make a regular habit of fasting between one to three days from time to time. This will keep your spirit sharp, and your faith at peak condition, so that you can be fruitful in every good work. "So that you may live a life worthy of the Lord and please Him in every way: bearing fruit in every good work, growing in the knowledge of God." (Colossians 1:10)

Some people are put off fasting because they fear they might harm themselves physically. There is no danger whatsoever in moderate fasting for the average person. Indeed, fasting for a few days up to five days has physical benefits in its own right. The body gets a well-deserved rest from digesting and assimilating food and has a chance to do a thorough cleaning up operation, getting rid of excess fat, and poisonous residues in the blood.

Some people have fasted for forty days. For the normal spiritual exercise, however, one to four days seem sensible. By four days I mean complete four days without food or any nourishing drink, and not breaking to eat every night. In my opinion it defeats the purpose if one drinks tea or orange juice during a fast. Most people find it easier to fast if only water is taken throughout.

It is essential to drink water, as the body needs it to dilute the toxic substances excreted during a long fast. Also drinking water minimizes the problem of dehydration. One should drink plenty of water, at least two pints a day. It is advisable to start gently by fasting for one day only if one is a beginner. Using the weapon of fasting and prayer against the forces of Satan is by no means limited to casting out Devils and healing the sick. Don't be tempted to stand in the wings and all this casting out of Devils is not for you. Demons operate in practically every facet of life. Satan is the author of all confusion and evil, and he must be challenged. The Devil is out to destroy homes, domestic and private lives, parent/child relationship, husband/wife relationship, business, or church life. He must not be allowed to have his own way.

One family who discovered that their daughter, who had professed conversion, took an unsaved boyfriend and was proving difficult at home, went to the Lord with prayer and fasting. The man and his wife fasted for five days, resisting the Devil over their precious daughter. Within a short while she gave up the boy, and they did not even talk to her about it. You cannot sit around and allow the Devil to rob you of joy, happiness, and your God-given prosperity without resisting him. Don't let him push you around, stay your ground and stand up to him by prayer and fasting.

16. POWER from ON HIGH

Before Jesus ascended, he left his disciples strict instructions: "I am going to send you what my Father has promised; but stay in the city until you have been clothed with power from on high." (Luke 24:49) They were to wait in Jerusalem until the day of Pentecost, when the Holy Spirit would come. When they had received power through the Holy Spirit, they were to go into all the world and preach the gospel.

No one can do miracles or expect to exercise authority over the Devils without the baptism of the Holy Spirit. Even Jesus did not begin his public ministry until after the Holy Spirit had come upon Him at his baptism in the river Jordan. Peter says of Him, "how God anointed Jesus of Nazareth with the Holy Spirit and power, and how he went around doing good and healing all who were under the power of the Devil, because God was with Him." (Acts 10:38)

When the Pharisees accused Jesus of casting out demons by the prince of demons, Beelzebub, he pointed out that it was by the power of the Holy Spirit that he was doing it. "And if I drive out demons by Beelzebul, by whom do your people drive them out? So then, they will be your judges. But if it is by the Spirit of God that I drive out demons, then the kingdom of God has come upon you." (Matthew 12:27, 28)

The infilling of the Holy Spirit is power for service, so that an ordinary Christian can live the victorious life, enjoy his rights in Christ, take authority over Devils, pray effectively, and worship with greater liberty. "Be filed with the Spirit." (Ephesians 5:18)

The Powerful Name of Jesus

"Therefore, God exalted Him to the highest place and gave Him the name that is above every name, that at the name of Jesus every knee should bow, in heaven and on earth and under the earth." (Philippians 2:9, 10) When a Christian loves the Lord, is free from demonic contaminations, knows his rights in Christ, is full of faith and the Holy Spirit, he is ready to effectively use the name of Jesus against the Devil. Jesus says, "In My Name shall they cast out Devils." (Mark 16:17) Jesus wants us to use his name. By using His Name in faith, it is as if He Himself were there doing the works in person. Whatever challenges face us, when we use the Name, the challenges become his. Through His Name on our lips Jesus takes over. The Devils know and respect the Name of Jesus. It is a Name they must obey.

The Safety of the Believer

If a Christian stands on redemption ground and does not go beyond the protection of the blood of Jesus, there is no harm whatsoever that demons can do to him. As a Christian you are safe from demon possession because you are a temple of the Holy Spirit. For those who suffer from depression, oppression, and other afflictions of the Devil, there is deliverance through the prayer of faith in the name of Jesus. I am fully convinced that no demon in hell can lay a finger on the child of God. You are safe and secure in Christ. However, care must be taken not to allow a chink in your armor to let the enemy through. A gap in the armor is made if you permit sin, unbelief, an unforgiving spirit, resentment, or fear, room in your life. Past areas of compromise with the Devil should be dealt with. You too can say like Jesus our Lord, "I will not say much more to you, for the prince of this world is coming. He has no hold over me." (John 14:30)

Wonderful Discovery

If you would like to know Jesus as your personal Lord and Savior, take the following six simple steps:

Acknowledge

Romans 3:23: "For all have sinned and fall short of the glory of God." Luke 18:13: "But the tax collector stood at a distance. He would not even look up to heaven, but beat his breast and said, 'God, have mercy on me, a sinner.'" You must acknowledge in the light of God's word that you are a sinner.

Repent

Luke 13:3: "But unless you repent, you too will all perish." Repent means that you agree with God about your sin, and you are sorry enough to change your ways.

Confess

1 John 1:9: "If we confess our sins, he is faithful and just and will forgive us our sins and purify us from all unrighteousness." Romans 10:10: "The thief comes only to steal and kill and destroy; I have come that they may have life and have it to the full." Confess to God the fact that you are a sinner, who has broken his law.

Forsake

Isaiah 55:7: "Let the wicked forsake their ways and the unrighteous their thoughts. Let them turn to the Lord, and He will have mercy on them, and to our God, for He will freely pardon." It is no good confessing sins only to go back into them again. You must confess and forsake. You must make up your mind that you will have nothing more to do with a sinful way of life.

Believe

John 3:16: "For God so loved the world that he gave his one and only Son, that whoever believes in Him shall not perish but have eternal life." Romans 10:9: "If you declare with your mouth, 'Jesus is Lord,' and believe in your heart that God raised Him from the dead, you will be saved." When Jesus died on the cross it was for you. Believe that it was your sin he took away. He said, "It is finished." This means there is nothing more you have to do to be saved. Only believe.

Receive

John 1:11, 12: "He came to that which was his own, but his own did not receive Him. Yet to all who did receive Him, to those who believed in his name, he gave the right to become children of God." Revelation 3:20: Jesus is standing by the door of your heart right now. Why not ask Him in?

You can pray this prayer:

"Lord God, I ask you to forgive my sins through the blood of Jesus Christ. I ask You to come into my life. I give myself to you. Thank You for hearing me. In Jesus Name, Amen." If you prayed this prayer sincerely you are now a new creation in Christ Jesus, and the angels in heaven are rejoicing over you. Hallelujah!

About the Author

REV. (DR) PAUL JINADU
GENERAL OVERSEER

Rev. Dr. Paul Jinadu was born a Muslim in Lagos, Nigeria. He became a Christian after Jesus appeared to him, and he then abandoned his pursuit of a medical education in the United Kingdom. He went to The Bible College of Wales, Swansea in 1962 and later also studied theology at The London Bible College, where he graduated in 1972. He married Kate who he met in Bible College, and they returned to Nigeria as Missionaries in 1966. They first worked with the Apostolic Church in Lagos, and then extensively with the Foursquare Gospel Church as pastors and church planters.

They returned to the UK in the early 80's, with Paul going all over the country as a travelling evangelist and conference speaker. Kate, meanwhile, was involved in leading people to Christ through The Christian Coffee Club in York.

In 1985, at the invitation of many of his disciples, Paul started the New Covenant Church in Nigeria, and a year later in the UK. He now oversees over 600 branches of the church in 23 nations of the world. Paul was the second President of the African and Caribbean Evangelical Alliance in the UK. He is an Apostle, spiritual father, and mentor to many pastors across the globe; a sought-after speaker and author of, *I Have Seen the Lord,* and many other books. He conducts leadership seminars and training all over the world.

For more information:

New Covenant Church
www.newcovenantchurchnigeria.org

New Covenant Church Logistics
9606 East Foothill Blvd.
Rancho Cucamonga, CA 91730
(909) 791-8095
www.nccworld.org
info@nccworld.org

Made in the USA
Middletown, DE
27 June 2023

33951441R00051